HISTORY'S GREATEST RIVALS

AL CAPONE Vs. ELIOT NESS

OPPOSITE SIDES OF THE LAW

Ellis Roxburgh

Gareth Stevens
PUBLISHING

Please visit our website, **www.garethstevens.com**. For a free color catalog of all our high-quality books, call toll-free 1-800-542-2595 or fax 1-877-542-2596.

Library of Congress Cataloging-in-Publication Data

Roxburgh, Ellis.
Al Capone vs. Eliot Ness: opposite sides of the law / by Ellis Roxburgh.
p. cm. — (History's greatest rivals)
Includes index.
ISBN 978-1-4824-2210-8 (pbk.)
ISBN 978-1-4824-2211-5 (6-pack)
ISBN 978-1-4824-2209-2 (library binding)
1. Capone, Al, 1899-1947 — Juvenile literature. 2. Ness, Eliot. 3. Gangsters — Illinois — Chicago — History —
20th century — Juvenile literature. 4. Organized crime — Illinois — Chicago — History — Juvenile literature.
5. Detectives — Illinois — Chicago. 6. Law enforcement — Illinois — Chicago — History. I. Roxburgh, Ellis.
II. Title.
HV6248.C17 R59 2015
364.1092—d23

Published in 2015 by
Gareth Stevens Publishing
111 East 14th Street, Suite 349
New York, NY 10003

© 2015 Brown Bear Books Ltd

For Brown Bear Books Ltd:
Editorial Director: Lindsey Lowe
Managing Editor: Tim Cooke
Children's Publisher: Anne O'Daly
Design Manager: Keith Davis
Designer: Lynne Lennon
Picture Manager: Sophie Mortimer

Picture Credits
Front Cover: Corbis: Bettmann left; Library of Congress: right; Shutterstock: background. Alamy: Everett
Collection Historical 20, J.D, Fisher 39; Corbis: Bettmann 4, 14, 22, 26, 29, 38, 43; Getty Images: Chicago
History Museum 13, 33, Gamma-Keystone 23, New York Daily News Archives 9, 21, Popperfoto 28; Library of
Congress: 5, 6, 8, 12, 15, 16, 17, 18, 19, 27, 30, 31, 32, 40, 44, 45; Mary Evans Picture Library: Everett Collection 41,
Ronald Grant Archive 35; Robert Hunt Library: ifc, 10, 35; Shutterstock: 4/5, 24 36, 37, 42/43; U.S. National
Archives: 7, 11, 34. Artistic Effects Shutterstock

Manufactured in the United States of America

CPSIA compliance information: Batch #CW15GS. For further information contact Gareth Stevens, New York, New York at 1-800-542-2595.

CONTENTS

AT ODDS

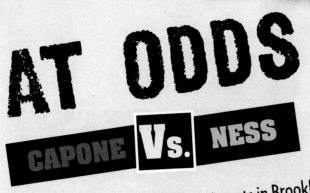

Born of Italian immigrants in Brooklyn, New York, Al Capone (1899–1947) was the most feared gangster in America in the 1920s.

* Capone controlled a crime network said to earn $75 million a year.

* Capone did not finish high school. Instead, he went to work for a local gangster.

* Capone loved attention and wore custom-made, brightly colored suits.

* After being wounded in a fight, Capone was nicknamed "Scarface."

* Capone was a violent man. He is said to have clubbed three enemies to death with a baseball bat.

Born of Norwegian immigrants in Chicago, Illinois, Eliot Ness (1903–1957) was a quiet man who became one of the 20th century's most effective law enforcement officers.

* Ness earned only around $2,500 a year working for the Bureau of Prohibition.

* Ness was an able student who earned a master's degree in criminology.

* Ness dressed in the kind of plain suits he could afford on his salary.

* Ness was tall and slim, with piercing blue eyes.

* Ness was well known for always controlling his temper.

* Ness was committed to upholding the law, even when he understood that the Prohibition laws were very unpopular.

CONTEXT

The Eighteenth Amendment that came into effect in January 1920 banned the sale of alcohol. An unexpected result of the new law was a sudden growth in organized crime during the 1920s.

In the 19th century, many Americans felt that drinking was destroying people's lives. Women were particularly concerned that men drank so much they became poor husbands and fathers. In 1830, the average adult American drank the equivalent of 7 gallons of pure alcohol a year—about three times the amount people drink today. The temperance, or anti-alcohol, movement started in the 1830s, when Protestant churches began to ask people to drink in moderation. This campaign had little effect so, after the end of the Civil War in 1865, the movement began to call for people to stop drinking completely.

Prohibition Arrives

On January 16, 1920, the Eighteenth Amendment to the US Constitution came

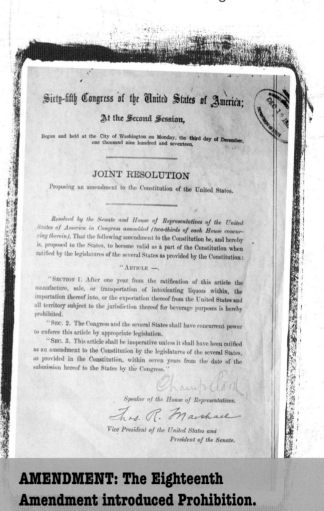

AMENDMENT: The Eighteenth Amendment introduced Prohibition.

LIQUOR: A warehouse full of illegal liquor during Prohibition.

into effect. It prohibited the sale and manufacture of alcohol. Drinking alcohol, however, remained legal, and there was great demand for drink. Criminals soon began to illegally produce and distribute alcohol. There was so much money to be made that some gangsters became extremely rich and powerful.

Chicago

The focus of most crime was the cities, particularly New York and Chicago. By 1920, Chicago had a population of 3 million and was the second largest city in the country. It was a relatively new city, and its local government was known to be corrupt,

> " We have seen the evil of the manufacture and sale of intoxicating liquors in our midst; let us try prohibition and see what this will do for us. "
>
> Thomas Jordan Jarvis, 1908

> ❝ **I'm only a second-hand furniture dealer.** ❞
>
> **Al Capone, 1920**

especially under Mayor "Big Bill" Thompson, who was elected in 1915. Virtually everyone in public service took bribes, even the police. This made Chicago highly attractive to criminals such as James "Big Jim" Colosimo, who led Chicago's main crime syndicate at the start of the 1920s.

Capone Moves to Chicago

Colosimo could see that Prohibition was a chance to make money. To help him expand into the liquor trade, he brought in a gangster from New York named Johnny Torrio, who became his right-hand man. Torrio soon sent for one of the men who had worked for him in New York: Al Capone. Capone moved to Chicago, where he worked as a bouncer in one of Colosimo's illegal clubs.

OFFICIAL: W. A. Green was chief prohibition inspector.

BAR: People drank liquor in disguised bars known as speakeasies.

Getting to the Top

Before long, Torrio was running Colosimo's businesses. When Colosimo was gunned down and killed in 1920, Torrio was widely thought to be behind the murder. Torrio was now Chicago's most powerful gangster. Soon his empire included thousands of illegal bars, known as speakeasies, nightclubs, and gambling dens. His job was made much easier because Mayor Thompson was not interested in enforcing the Prohibition laws.

Torrio chose Al Capone to run his empire; Capone was just 22 years old, but he was clearly smart. While he was running Torrio's illegal businesses, he said he was a second-hand furniture dealer—although he never sold any furniture.

AL CAPONE

Al Capone rose from being a Brooklyn errand boy to become the biggest gangster in America. He believed he was above the law.

Alphonse Capone was the fourth child of Italian immigrants. As a teenager, he was known for his temper, and he never finished school. Instead, he was employed by a local gangster named Johnny Torrio.

Move to Chicago

When Torrio moved to Chicago to cash in on the expanding illegal liquor business, he sent for Capone to join him. Capone helped Torrio create the biggest Italian organized crime gang in the city. When a rival gang tried to kill Torrio in 1925, Torrio fled to Italy. Aged just 26, Capone was now boss of the organization.

MUGSHOT: A knife wound on his left cheek earned Capone the nickname "Scarface."

CHARITY: Capone made himself popular with some people in Chicago by running a soup kitchen.

Expansion of Crime

Capone oversaw the expansion of the gang's illegal activities. He also ruthlessly eliminated his criminal rivals. His hoodlums were blamed for more than 300 murders. He made a fortune and bought a luxury mansion in Florida. He used part of his money to bribe law enforcement officials. He also paid voters and officials to achieve the reelection of Chicago's corrupt mayor, "Big Bill" Thompson, in 1927.

> " You can say what you want about Al Capone. If people were desperate and needed help, he was there to help them. He didn't expect anything in return and he never expected you to pay him back. "
>
> Italian–American, Chicago, c.1930

ELIOT NESS

Eliot Ness was a native of Chicago who became a government official and refused to be intimidated or bribed by anybody.

Eliot Ness was the youngest of five children born to Norwegian immigrants in Chicago. A good student, Ness studied economics at the University of Chicago and later earned a master's degree in criminal justice. Ness's parents were disappointed when he took his first job in 1925, joining the Retail Credit Company as an investigator. They thought the job was not good enough for such a well-educated man, but it proved valuable experience for Ness's next job. In 1927, he got himself a job at the Chicago Treasury Department.

HONEST: Ness soon marked himself out by his refusal to be bribed.

Prohibition Bureau

With the help of his brother-in-law, Ness won a transfer to the Prohibition Bureau in 1928. This was a federal agency within the Bureau of Internal Revenue (later the Internal Revenue Service, or IRS) responsible for enforcing the Prohibition laws.

ARMED: Police work in the 1920s was highly dangerous. Both police and criminals were armed.

At the time Ness joined, the Prohibition Bureau was known to be highly corrupt. Its officers often took bribes from criminals. Capone's organization was said to use nearly one-third of its profits to pay off corrupt policemen and officials. Ness was one of the few officers who refused to be bribed.

> **If you don't like action and excitement, you don't go into police work.**
>
> **Elliot Ness, 1957**

Reputation for Honesty

Ness's reputation for honesty brought him to the attention of his bosses, who asked him to put together a small group that could fight Capone and his illegal trade. Ness eventually selected nine men from a possible 150. Their honesty and refusal to take bribes led to them becoming known as "The Untouchables."

CAPONE'S MOB

To survive in Chicago's murderous gangland in the 1920s, Al Capone surrounded himself with mobsters he could trust.

Chicago had an estimated 1,300 gangs by the middle of the 1920s. As law enforcement tried to stamp out their activities, the gangs fought each other for control. Capone surrounded himself with trusted Italian immigrants from Naples, where his family came from. His first boss, Johnny Torrio, was also from Naples.

GANGSTERS: Capone (bottom left) was only one of the gang leaders in Chicago.

CORRUPT: "Big Bill" Thompson was the corrupt mayor of Chicago.

Two of Capone's closest associates were his brothers, Frank and Ralph. Al was particularly close to Frank, who was gunned down by the police on April 1, 1924. Ralph "Bottles" Capone ran Capone's beer-bottling companies. He was the front man of the Chicago mob until he was jailed for tax evasion in 1932.

Italian Gangsters

Capone bought the loyalty of his hoodlums through fear. If they crossed him, he had them killed. He also used bribes to buy the loyalty of officials such as Mayor Thompson. Some Chicagoans saw him as a modern-day Robin Hood, because he helped the poor by paying for a soup kitchen. He was a popular celebrity at ball games and restaurants, where he was known for handing out huge tips.

" You never get no back talk from a corpse. "

Frank Capone, 1925

CRIME FIGHTERS

Eliot Ness was one of a new breed of law enforcement officials and local politicians who were determined to stand up to criminals.

Many Americans were shocked by the rise in crime in the early 1920s. The authorities seemed too corrupt to react. But things were changing. In Washington, DC, the Bureau of Investigation—later known as the Federal Bureau of Investigation—came under the control of a new director, J. Edgar Hoover. Like Ness, Hoover was determined to make crime fighting less corrupt. Meanwhile the Prohibition Bureau also hired more professional agents, such as Izzy Einstein and Moe Smith, who made a record 4,392 arrests.

DIRECTOR: J. Edgar Hoover cleaned up the Bureau of Investigation.

An Honest Mayor

There were also changes in Chicago, where William E. Dever was elected mayor in 1923. Unlike the corrupt former mayor, "Big Bill" Thompson, Dever was determined to enforce Prohibition. In 1927, however, he lost the mayoral election again to Thompson, whose campaign had been largely funded by Al Capone.

AGENTS: Izzy Einstein and Moe Smith went around the country on the trail of illegal liquor businesses.

The Secret Six

Ness's brother-in-law, Alexander Jamie, was the Chief Special Agent in the Department of Justice. He helped get Ness his special commission within the Prohibition Bureau. In 1930, Jamie helped organize six influential businessmen to fund operations against Al Capone. Known as the Secret Six, they bought information and set up false businesses to gather information about Capone's gang. Ness was a great admirer of these six mysterious men.

> " These six men were gambling with their lives, unarmed, to accomplish what three thousand police and three hundred prohibition agents had failed miserably to accomplish. "

Eliot Ness on the Secret Six, 1957

LINES ARE DRAWN

Al Capone's rise in Chicago's gangland brought him into conflict with other gangsters—and eventually with the US authorities.

Capone's was not the only criminal gang in Chicago. Other gangs controlled different parts of the city. From 1923 to 1927, when Mayor William Dever had enforced Prohibition, Capone and his rivals began fighting over territory as their profits fell. The "beer wars" saw a huge increase in murders between the gangs. One of Capone's biggest rivals was the Irish gang leader, "Bugs" Moran.

Capone's problems increased still further in late 1927. Mike Hughes, the new Chicago chief of police, announced a crackdown on the activities of the gangs. Capone was furious and told the press he was

RAID: Watched carefully by the police, agents pour illegal liquor away after a raid.

PRESIDENT: Herbert Hoover, who became president in 1929, wanted Capone jailed.

sick of Chicago and promptly left the city to go and live in a luxury villa in Miami. With Capone no longer around to control the rival gangs, Chicago became even more lawless than before.

> **"** Public service is my motto. Ninety percent of the people of Cook County drink and gamble and my offense has been to furnish them with those amusements. **"**

Al Capone, 1929

Back Home

Capone had become so important to the running of Chicago that he could not stay at his new Miami home for long. As the 1928 presidential election approached, the Chicago Crime Commission asked Capone to return to the city in order to ensure that no one tried to use bribes to rig the election result. Capone did so, and Herbert Hoover was elected president.

St. Valentine's Day Massacre

Meanwhile, Capone's feud with the North Side gang run by "Bugs" Moran was still going on. Capone had survived numerous assassination attempts by Moran's men. To show his rivals who was boss, Capone came up with a plan to get rid of Moran's gang.

Capone's men lured the other gang to a warehouse with the false promise of a new supply of cheap whiskey. As Moran's men waited, a carload of men in police uniforms arrived. The gangsters assumed the newcomers were corrupt policemen who were in on the deal. In fact, they were Capone's men in disguise. They lined up the gangsters against the wall and killed them all using machine guns. (Moran survived, because he arrived late for the meeting.) No one was ever arrested for the massacre, which took its name from the date: St. Valentine's Day, February 14, 1929.

RIVAL: "Bugs" Moran survived the massacre.

After the Massacre

Capone was widely known to have been behind the massacre, but there was not enough evidence to convict him. Capone now believed he had shown that he was the toughest gangster of all time. Unknown to him, however, changes in government meant that his time at the top was already running out.

POLICE: Chicago police re-create the scene of the St. Valentine's Day Massacre.

A New President

Three weeks after the massacre, Herbert Hoover was inaugurated as president. According to some accounts, Hoover had been a guest of the businessman J. C. Penney in Miami, when they were disturbed by noise from Capone's neighboring estate. Hoover vowed then to end Capone's career. More likely, Hoover was disturbed at the open way in which Capone broke the law and brought violence to the streets of one of America's biggest cities. Soon after Hoover took office, he ordered his Secretary of the Treasury, Andrew Mellon, to use the Internal Revenue Service and the Prohibition Bureau to stop Capone's illegal activities.

" Have you got this fellow Capone, yet? I want that man in jail. "

Herbert Hoover to Secretary of the Treasury Andrew Mellon, March 1929

THE UNTOUCHABLES

The federal government and state officials in Chicago decided that something had to be done about Capone's criminal activities.

The only question was what? Capone had bribed almost all the officials who might interfere with or prevent him making money. Meanwhile, the different branches of the law—the police, the Prohibition Bureau, the FBI—did not work together, so they did not share any useful information about Capone's many illegal activities.

In 1929, for the first time, US Attorney George Johnson urged the various government agencies to pool their information about Capone. Johnson hired Eliot Ness to head up the Prohibition team.

STILL: One of Ness's targets was the equipment used to manufacture liquor.

MOBSTERS: It was often difficult to get witnesses to identify criminals.

Just as significantly, Johnson hired a smart tax inspector named Frank Wilson. Johnson asked Wilson to look into Capone's tax affairs, which he believed were bound to be illegal.

Finding the Recruits

When Johnson hired him, Ness was still only in his mid-20s. His first task was to recruit a team to work with him who would be as honest as he was. It was a tough challenge. Ness sifted through the resumes of hundreds of Prohibition officers before he drew up a short list of 50 men. From those 50, he used strict criteria to reduce the list to just

> **" We had undertaken what might be a suicidal mission. "**
>
> **Eliot Ness, 1957**

15 possible candidates. They had to be males under 30 years, and they had to be single. They had to be honest, but they also had to possess a useful skill, such as being a good driver, or able to tap telephones to intercept conversations, or be a skilled marksman. From the list of 15 men chosen, just nine made the final cut. The Prohibition Bureau hailed them as "the Untouchables," because they could not be bribed.

Who Were the Untouchables?

The men Ness chose came from all walks of life and different parts of the country. He chose Barney Cloonan and Bill Gardner for their enormous size and strength—they were both huge. Ness did not follow football, so he did not realize that Gardner was a former football star. Ness intended Gardner to work undercover until someone pointed out that everyone would recognize him. At 50, Gardner was also much older than the other Untouchables.

Ness chose Mike King, an unassuming man, to be the facts man who would organize the Untouchables' strategy. Lyle Chapman could solve problems

> I felt a chill foreboding for my men as I envisioned the violent reaction we would produce in the criminal octopus hovering over Chicago.
>
> Eliot Ness, 1957

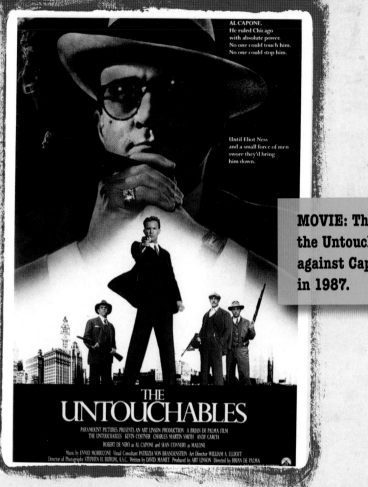

AL CAPONE.
He ruled Chicago
with absolute power.
No one could touch him.
No one could stop him.

Until Eliot Ness
and a small force of men
swore they'd bring
him down.

THE
UNTOUCHABLES

PARAMOUNT PICTURES PRESENTS AN ART LINSON PRODUCTION A BRIAN DE PALMA FILM
THE UNTOUCHABLES KEVIN COSTNER CHARLES MARTIN SMITH ANDY GARCIA
ROBERT DE NIRO as AL CAPONE and SEAN CONNERY as MALONE
Music by ENNIO MORRICONE Visual Consultant PATRIZIA VON BRANDENSTEIN Art Director WILLIAM A. ELLIOTT
Director of Photography STEPHEN H. BURUM, A.S.C. Written by DAVID MAMET Produced by ART LINSON Directed by BRIAN DE PALMA

MOVIE: This movie about the Untouchables' fight against Capone was made in 1987.

and had the added bonus of being fit and strong. Paul Robsky's special skill was tapping telephones. This was how the Untouchables got information about Capone's activities. Tom Friel was from Pennsylvania, where he worked as a state trooper, while Joe Leeson could trail an automobile without being spotted. Sam Seager had been a guard on death row at the infamous Sing Sing jail in New York.

As his deputy, Ness chose Marty Lahart. Lahart had worked with Ness in Chicago and was another strong, fit man. The team was ready to go into action.

NESS'S RAIDS

Ness was ready to take on Al Capone. From late 1927, he targeted the heart of Capone's business: the whiskey stills.

Ness decided to begin by showing Capone just what the Prohibition Bureau could do. He came up with a plan to shut down 18 of Capone's illegal stills in the Chicago Heights district in just one night. Each of the Untouchables took some Prohibition agents and targeted one or two stills. To make sure none of the Prohibition agents could warn Capone about what was going to happen, they were only told of the plan at the last minute.

The Untouchables spent hours working out their strategy for the night. Each still would be raided at the same time—9:30 P.M.—so that the raids would be over before the gangsters had time to react.

SPEAKEASY: Illegal drinking dens were known as speakeasies.

The Cozy Corners

Eliot Ness's own target for the raids was the Cozy Corners Saloon. It was at the heart of Capone's Chicago Heights operation,

RAID: Agents destroyed any
bootleg liquor they found.

which supplied liquor not just to Chicago but also across the whole
Midwest. Ness was determined to show everyone how serious he
was about stamping out Capone's illegal business. Rushing into the
saloon holding sawn-off shotguns, Ness and his men shut down the
speakeasy and a large part of Capone's operation at the same time.

A Good Night's Work

Across Chicago Heights,
it was the same story. The
Untouchables had scored a
massive victory in their fight
against organized crime, closing
down 18 stills and arresting 52
men in one night. But for Ness,
this was just the start.

> " Everybody keep
> his place! This is a
> federal raid! "

Eliot Ness raids the Cozy Corners, 1929

CAPONE FIGHTS BACK

Ness's raids infuriated Capone, who was determined to stop Ness from destroying both his business and his power and livelihood.

After the Cozy Corners raids, Ness targeted Capone's breweries. These were where Capone made most of his money by brewing illegal beer. To catch Capone's men red-handed, Ness used a massive flat-bed truck with a reinforced steel bumper on its front to break through the brewery doors. After some gangsters escaped by climbing onto a roof, the truck also carried scaling ladders. In the first 6 months of operation, Ness and the Untouchables closed down 19 breweries worth around a million dollars.

FOOTBALL: Capone (right) sits in the front row of a football game in October 1931.

RELAXED: Al Capone fishes off the back of his luxury yacht in 1928.

Capone was convinced he could bribe the Untouchables. Even Ness, their leader, earned only around $2,500 a year. Capone had one of his men offer Ness $2,000 a week to stop the raids. Capone made the same offer to Lahart and Seager. All three men turned him down.

Death Threats

Even men who could not be bribed could be scared or killed, even though Capone knew that killing federal agents would cause serious trouble. Ness survived three attempts on his life and many death threats. His friend and driver, Frank Basile, was not so lucky. He was murdered in December 1928. Ness identified the body and promised to avenge his death.

> " I got a message for you. You've had your last chance to be smart. Just keep in mind that sometime soon you're going to be found lying in a ditch with a hole in your head. "

Anonymous message to Ness

NESS'S PARADE

The murder of Frank Basile in December 1928 inspired Eliot Ness's most outrageous plan to show Al Capone who was now boss.

Ness was more determined than ever to humiliate Capone and have him sent to jail. In early 1929, the Untouchables carried out a number of successful raids on Capone's operations, although other raids had failed when Capone's men were tipped off.

During the raids, Ness had confiscated some 45 vehicles belonging to Capone. They were all shapes and sizes and were all almost brand new. They were being stored at a government garage, but were due

CHASE: Gangster vehicles were sometimes seized after a police chase.

to be moved. That gave Ness an idea. He ordered the vehicles be cleaned until they shone. Then he called Capone on the telephone at his base in the Lexington Hotel.

Taunting Capone

Calling the startled gangster "Snorkey," a nickname that only those closest to Capone were allowed to use, Ness told him to look out of his window at precisely 11:00 A.M. When Capone looked out onto Michigan Avenue, he saw a convoy of his confiscated vehicles slowly driving along the street.

Capone was furious. Not only had Ness severely dented his profits, he was now publicly humiliating him. The gangster stormed through the hotel rooms, smashing everything with a baseball bat.

> **What we had done this day was enrage the bloodiest mob in criminal history.**
>
> **Eliot Ness, date 1957**

CAPONE ON TRIAL

Ness had succeeded in scaring Capone, but in the end it was the Internal Revenue Service that defeated Chicago's most famous gangster.

While Eliot Ness was showing Capone and Chicago what he and his honest Untouchables could do, other federal agents led by Frank Wilson had been quietly working away behind the scenes. Their patient paperwork would eventually bring its reward.

Where's the Money?

Al Capone enjoyed a lavish lifestyle. His extravagance was clear for everyone to see. He wore diamond-studded belts, silk shirts, and custom-made suits. He was known to be a generous tipper. When the Great Depression hit Chicago in 1929, he paid for a soup kitchen to feed the unemployed. He ran up telephone bills of $39,000.

MONEY: Frank Wilson followed the trail of Capone's money.

On paper, however, Capone had no income. There was no record of him earning money or paying taxes. Although estimates suggested that Capone was worth around $30 million in 1929, he had

COURT: Al Capone (second left) attends court with his legal team.

never filed a tax return. The federal case against Capone was helped by a 1927 Supreme Court ruling that said that even money that was illegally earned was liable for taxes.

Checking the Records

Frank Wilson and five other Treasury investigators combed through every financial record they could find to prove that Capone was the

> **Every time a boy falls off a tricycle, every time a black cat has gray kittens, every time someone stubs a toe, every time there's a murder or a fire or the marines land in Nicaragua, the police and the newspapers holler 'Get Capone!'**
>
> **Al Capone, 1930**

> **"** If the United States government thinks it can clean up Chicago by sending me to jail, well, it's all right with me. I guess maybe I owe the government this stretch in jail, anyway. **"**

Al Capone, March 1931

VERDICT: The signatures of the jury on the court's guilty verdict.

head of an organization that earned millions of dollars. By 1930, the investigators had gathered enough information to make their move.

On March 13, 1931, a grand jury indicted Al Capone on one charge of evading federal income taxes in 1924. Two months later, they added more charges for the years 1925 to 1929. But Capone's lawyers thought they could negotiate a short prison term in return for a guilty plea and the district attorney seemed willing to agree.

A Shock for Capone

Capone appeared in court on June 18, 1931, in front of Judge James H. Wilkerson and pleaded guilty. He expected to be sentenced to just two and a half years in jail. He was in for a shock. Judge Wilkerson adjourned the court until July 30 while he considered the plea.

Back to Court

On July 30, Capone was back in court wearing a pea-green suit. To his shock, Wilkerson announced that he would not accept the guilty plea. This meant that Capone would have to stand trial after all. The gangster had prepared for this possibility, however. His men had started to bribe members of the jury in order to get Capone found not guilty if there was a full trial.

But the judge had another shock in store for Capone. To make sure there was no corruption, Wilkerson dismissed the jury and replaced them with a new group of jurors. Capone's men had no chance to bribe these new jurors.

Trial and Sentence

The trial finally opened on October 5, 1931. The prosecution called many witnesses to make the case against Capone. The defense meanwhile tried to make out that he was nothing more than a gambler.

The jury did not believe the defense case. On October 18, 1931, they found Capone guilty of tax evasion.

MUGSHOT: Capone spent 11 years in prison.

DEATH OF CAPONE

Capone's criminal reign was at an end thanks to the bravery of Ness and his men, Frank Wilson, and Judge Wilkerson.

On October 18, 1931, the jury found Capone guilty of tax evasion. Six days later, Judge Wilkerson sentenced Capone to 11 years in prison. It was the longest sentence ever awarded for tax evasion.

Capone still refused to believe that he had finally been brought to justice. He thought he would overturn his sentence on appeal and avoid having to serve any time in jail. He was in for another shock.

CELL: Capone had already served a short prison sentence in 1929: he brought furniture for his cell.

THE ROCK: Alcatraz was on a rocky island, which made it nearly impossible to escape from.

Life in Jail

Eliot Ness put Capone on a train to Atlanta, Georgia, where Capone was imprisoned in the penitentiary. Capone continued to run his businesses from his cell while his lawyers appealed. Now that the authorities had Capone behind bars, however, they were not going to let him go. Capone's appeals failed. When his illegal activities in jail became known in 1934, Capone was moved to Alcatraz Prison on an island in San Francisco Bay.

> " Well, I'm on my way to do eleven years. I've got to do it, that's all. I'm not sore at anybody. Some people are lucky. I wasn't. "

Al Capone to Eliot Ness, October 1931

Going Home

By the time he was released from jail in November 1939, Capone had suffered a mental breakdown. He returned home in poor health and with the mental age of a 12-year-old. He died on January 25, 1947, just after his 48th birthday.

A LIFE OF SERVICE

With Capone in jail, Eliot Ness was the toast of the United States. He was in great demand by other cities that also needed cleaning up.

From Chicago, Ness headed to Ohio. He was given the job of closing down illegal stills across the Appalachian Mountains of Kentucky, Tennessee, and Ohio. He succeeded in shutting them all down.

In November 1935, Harold Burton was elected as the new mayor of Cleveland, Ohio. At the time, Cleveland was the second most lawless city in America after Chicago.

AWARD: Ness (left) receives an award for improving traffic safety in Cleveland in April 1940.

GRAVE: Eliot Ness, his wife, Elizabeth, and his son, Robert, are buried in Cleveland, Ohio.

Safety Director

Despite the fact that Ness was not a local man and was still only 33 years old, Burton hired him as his new Safety Director. Ness set about cleaning up Cleveland's police and fire departments and improving morale. He reduced organized crime and gambling in the city. He even reorganized the city roads to make them safer.

> " I am not going to be a remote director. I am going to be out, and I'll cover this town pretty well. "
>
> **Eliot Ness, Cleveland, 1935**

Health Problems

Despite his successes at work, Ness's personal life was a disaster. He drank so much that in the end he was forced to resign from his job. He died from alcoholism in 1957, just a month before the publication of his widely successful account of his Chicago days, *The Untouchables*.

AFTERMATH

Al Capone had made it clear to Americans that Prohibition did not work. Eliot Ness, however, had shown that crime did not pay.

On December 5, 1933, the Twenty-First Amendment to the US Constitution was passed, overturning the ban on the sale and manufacture of alcohol. Even those who had campaigned for Prohibition could see that it had not worked. It had allowed criminals like Capone to make vast fortunes and to break the law for years.

OUTLAWS: Bonnie Parker and Clyde Barrow held up small-town banks in the heart of America during the early 1930s.

With the repeal of Prohibition, there were no longer huge profits to be made from liquor and crime organizations folded. Capone's jail sentence for tax evasion also showed that no one was safe from the Internal Revenue Service.

Law Enforcement

One major change that took place as a result of the battle between Eliot Ness and Al Capone was an

PRESSURE: The pressure to repeal Prohibition became irresistible.

increase in federal activity against criminals. It was based on the idea of US Attorney George Johnson that federal organizations pool information to catch Capone. The newly cleaned up Federal Bureau of Investigation (FBI) would work as a central organization to catch America's worst criminals.

New Types of Crime

Gang crime fell. Instead, the Depression of the 1930s saw outlaws such as Bonnie and Clyde, from Dallas, carry out small-town robberies. The era of Al Capone and the organized crime gangs was over.

> **Doubts raced through my mind as I considered the feasibility of enforcing a law which the majority of honest citizens didn't seem to want.**

Eliot Ness on Prohibition, 1956

41

JUDGMENT

CAPONE Vs. NESS

Who won the crime war? Ness dealt Capone some heavy blows, but it was the Internal Revenue Service that finally ended his criminal reign.

* Capone claimed to practice a kind of "capitalism," like any other businessman in the United States.

* He lived in great luxury, and had a reputation for helping others—but he was also probably responsible for at least 300 murders.

* Capone believed that anyone could be bought for the right price. Ness proved him wrong.

* Capone's reign, though infamous, was short. He was only at the top of Chicago's gangland for less than a decade.

Eliot Ness was the highest profile law officer to take on Al Capone. Despite the bravery and honesty of the Untouchables, however, careful paperwork behind the scenes would eventually bring Capone down.

* **Ness and his men caused serious financial damage by raiding Capone's businesses but could not close them down.**

* **Ness gained much positive publicity for Prohibition through his honesty.**

* **Even Ness admitted that Prohibition had little public support.**

* **In later life, Ness may have exaggerated his own role in Capone's downfall.**

* **Ness's personal life after Chicago was sad and ironically was cut short by alcohol abuse.**

TIMELINE

The Prohibition period that saw the rise of Al Capone was relatively brief. It was only toward the end of the 1920s that the US authorities became determined to stop illegal activities.

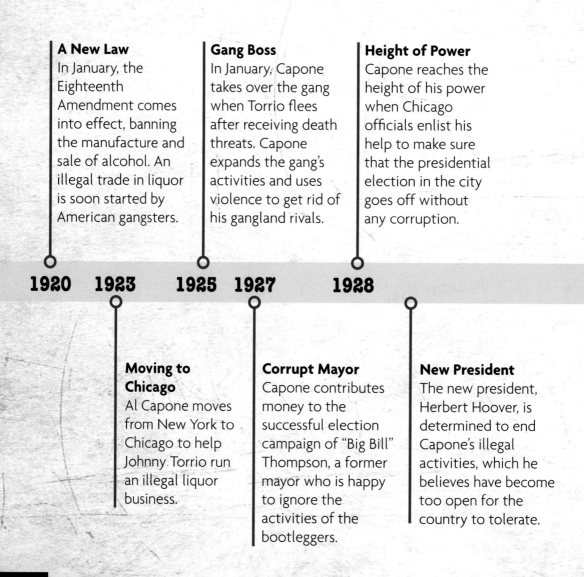

A New Law
In January, the Eighteenth Amendment comes into effect, banning the manufacture and sale of alcohol. An illegal trade in liquor is soon started by American gangsters.

Gang Boss
In January, Capone takes over the gang when Torrio flees after receiving death threats. Capone expands the gang's activities and uses violence to get rid of his gangland rivals.

Height of Power
Capone reaches the height of his power when Chicago officials enlist his help to make sure that the presidential election in the city goes off without any corruption.

1920   **1923**   **1925**   **1927**   **1928**

Moving to Chicago
Al Capone moves from New York to Chicago to help Johnny Torrio run an illegal liquor business.

Corrupt Mayor
Capone contributes money to the successful election campaign of "Big Bill" Thompson, a former mayor who is happy to ignore the activities of the bootleggers.

New President
The new president, Herbert Hoover, is determined to end Capone's illegal activities, which he believes have become too open for the country to tolerate.

Notorious Crime
On February 14, Capone's men carry out an infamous gangster crime, the St. Valentine's Day Massacre, when they gun down seven rival gang members.

High-Profile Raids
Ness's men use phone taps to gather information to carry out raids on Capone's illegal activities, seizing equipment and arresting Capone's men.

Director of Safety
In demand after his success in Chicago, Eliot Ness becomes director of safety in Cleveland, Ohio.

1929   **1931**   **1935 1939**

The Untouchables
With new orders from Hoover to get Capone, the Prohibition Bureau steps up its efforts. Agent Eliot Ness recruits a group of men he believes will reject Capone's efforts at bribery.

Into Court
In March, a grand jury finds that Capone should stand trial for tax evasion. Capone believes he will receive only a short sentence. Instead, at his trial in October, he is sentenced to 11 years in jail.

Rapid Decline
After his release from prison, Al Capone spends the next 8 years at his home in Florida. He is both physically and mentally weak, and is nursed by his family until his death in 1947.

GLOSSARY

bootlegger Someone who illegally makes, supplies, or sells alcohol.

brewery A place where beer is brewed.

bribe To dishonestly get someone to act in your favor by giving him or her money or other gifts.

confiscate To take away someone's possessions with official permission.

corrupt Describes someone who is willing to act dishonestly in return for personal gain.

gangster A member of a gang of violent criminals.

grand jury A jury, usually with 23 members, that examines how much evidence there is in order to take an accusation to trial.

hoodlum Someone involved in crime and violence.

ironically A word used to describe a situation in which the outcome is very different or opposite from what might be expected.

massacre The deliberate killing of a large number of people.

mob A term that describes the Italian Mafia or a similar criminal organization.

mobster A member of a gang of violent criminals.

organized crime An organization with proper management structures, the purpose of which is to make money from crime.

Prohibition The prevention by law of the manufacture and sale of alcohol between 1920 and 1933.

repeal To put aside a law so that it is no longer in force.

soup kitchen A place where free food is given to the poor or homeless.

speakeasy An illegal place for buying or drinking alcohol during Prohibition.

still A piece of equipment used in a distillery to manufacture alcoholic spirits.

syndicate A group of individuals or organizations acting together in their common interests.

temperance Abstaining from drinking alcohol.

FOR FURTHER INFORMATION

Books

Feinstein, Stephen. *The 1920s from Prohibition to Charles Lindbergh* (Decades of the 20th Century in Color). Enslow Publishers, 2006.

Forest, Christopher. *Gangs and Gangsters: Stories of Public Enemies* (Bad Guys). Velocity, 2010.

Gitlin, Martin. *The Prohibition Era* (Essential Events). ABDO Publishing Company, 2010.

Lindop, Edmund. *America in the 1920s* (20th-century America). 21st Century, 2010.

Matthews, Rupert, and Mark Bergin. *You Woudn't Want to be a Chicago Gangster!* Turtleback, 2010.

Schwartz, Heather E. *Gangsters, Bootleggers, and Bandits* (Shockzone—Villains). Lerner Publications, 2013.

Slavicek, Louise Chipley. *The Prohibition Era: Temperance in the United States* (Milestones in American History). Chelsea House Publishers, 2008.

Websites

www.fbi.gov/about-us/history/famous-cases/al-capone
Page on Al Capone from the official FBI website.

www.chicagohs.org/history/capone.html
A detailed biography of Al Capone from the Chicago Historical Society.

www.crimelibrary.com/gangsters_outlaws/cops_others/ness/1.html
Crime Library pages about Eliot Ness and his life fighting crime.

www.history.com/topics/al-capone
History.com pages about Al Capone, with many links and videos.

Publisher's note to educators and parents: Our editors have carefully reviewed these websites to ensure that they are suitable for students. Many websites change frequently, however, and we cannot guarantee that a site's future contents will continue to meet our high standards of quality and educational value. Be advised that students should be closely supervised whenever they access the Internet.

INDEX